GENTLE HAPPINESS

The Haiku of Japa

James Calb

Published May 2016 by Flying Squid

Visit James Calbraith's official website at
jamescalbraith.com
for the latest news, book details, and other information

Either as a crucial ingredient of the tea ceremony, an important element of shrine rituals, or simply as a way to cool oneself during the scorching Japanese summer, sweets are as central to Japanese life and culture as poetry or gardening.

To me, they have also been a way to experience this culture - and some of my best memories of Japan are in one way or another connected with its myriad snacks. One summer night, out of nowhere, I started writing haiku about these memories. I ended up with seventy little poems - enough to put together in this booklet.

1. Okashi

Poetry and sweets
What more does a wise man need
On this summer night

The first Japanese sweets were made from roasted chestnuts in the late Jomon period. The true confectionery was brought in from Tang China, together with Buddhism and classic poetry. Since then, the history of Japanese culture is inextricably joined with that of Japanese sweets. Through famine and prosperity, through war and peace, influenced by foreign traders and ancient traditions, the snack has become as much a symbol of Japan as cherry blossom, geisha - or haiku.

Wagashi — Traditional Japanese sweets

2. Jo-Namagashi — Nerikiri

Crimson maple leaf
Falls towards the tea tray —
Lands next to the cup

The "wet" tea ceremony snacks, namagashi, are the king of the Japanese sweets — and among them, Nerikiri is the Emperor. These are the tiny, colourful sculptures of soft dough that most people associate with the traditional Japanese confectionery. They are as seasonal and precious as Japanese poetry, little haiku made of rice flour and sugar.

3. Rakugan

Found in the attic
Who bought us this box of sweets?
The dust remembers

Pastel-coloured hard candy made from fine rice flour and refined sugar, and pressed into elaborate shapes in sculpted moulds, dry Rakugan keeps fresh for a long time, and is therefore among the favourite souvenirs from far-away travels.

. Yatsuhashi

The westerly winds
Bring the scents of distant lands —
Roof needs fixing again

This cinnamon-spiced sweet is a favourite of Kyoto, and comes in two forms. Baked and dried into the shape of a roof tile or cinnamon bark, or steamed "raw", a fluffy, soft parcel, wrapped around a pinch of sweet beans.

5. Nama Yatsuhashi

Letter from distant lands —
A tiny granule of home
Wrapped in soft blankets

True cinnamon arrived in Japan from India via China in 8th century, but it wasn't until late 17th century that a small teahouse near Shogoin Temple invented the Yatsuhashi. According to a recent survey, some 46% of visitors to Kyoto bring back home a souvenir of Yatsuhashi.

6. Hoshigaki

No time to rest!
Go check on the persimmons
A storm is coming

Hoshigaki — dried persimmons — are perhaps the most laborious of Japan's snacks. Picked in late Autumn, they are hung out to dry in the open air throughout winter. As they hang, each fruit is — gently! - massaged by hand every couple of days. The result, a chewy mass of sweet, aromatic, soft flesh, is well worth all that effort — and the extortionate price.

7. Kingyoku

Ah! Orchard in bloom
Call a painter to sketch it
Or a pastry chef

Tiny compositions of fruit, flowers and other items suspended in translucent agar jelly, the Kingyoku are frozen moments in time, three-dimensional edible photos, most popular in summer months as they are cool and refreshing both in taste and in appearance.

8. Hanakazura

Hush. A white heron
Fell asleep on thin ice
One step and it cracks

Hanakazura is a type of Kingyoku that most resembles thin, cracking ice, in which whole red beans were frozen. Agar jelly is a relatively modern invention, discovered in 17th century. Until then the Japanese, not allowed to eat animal products, had to make do with rough gelatine substitutes made from grains and beans.

9. Ukishima

Sunshine in the reeds
Writes letters on the shell of
A lazy turtle

Ukishima belongs to the tradition of wagashi named simply after what they most resemble. In this case, floating islands of reeds and peat, where the small pond turtles like to dwell. Other wagashi in this family include *Ishikoromo* - a white pebble, or *Kangori* - winter ice.

0. Kuri Kinton

Teahouse on the pass
The ringing bell announces
A fearful pilgrim

The confectionery made of pureed chestnuts and sweet potato is a specialty of Gifu Prefecture. This mountainous region is home to the Kiso Valley hiking trail, and a large population of black bears, which in summer months a wary traveller is supposed to keep at bay by ringing road-side bells.

11. Yubeshi

On a wind-swept coast
A single yuzu remains
Maiden's memory

Yubeshi is a specialty of the Noto Peninsula in Kaga region, a hollowed-out yuzu fruit stuffed with mochi dough and dried for six months in the wind. It played a crucial role in the romantic plot of the movie "A Tale of Samurai Cooking", a biography of Funaki Yasunobu, a famous chef and food writer from 18th c. Kaga.

12. Jiro Ame

Riches of Kaga —
Even the babies eat gold
Instead of milk

Another specialty of the Kaga region, Jiro Ame is a type of malt syrup, created from barley and rice. It's so nutritious, it was given to babies instead of mother's milk. The Maeda clan who ruled the Kaga Domain was at one point the second richest clan in Japan after the ruling Tokugawas, and their capital rivalled Kyoto and Edo in wealth and sophistication.

Mochi — Glutinous rice cakes

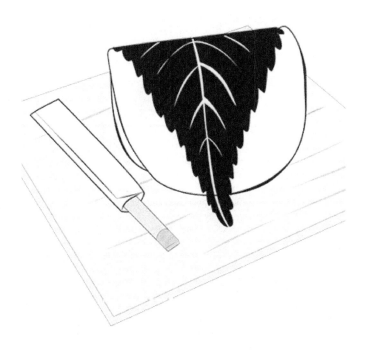

13. Kusamochi (mugwort mochi)

The city we build
Will last longer than others:
At least a century

Mochi, the glutinous rice balls, have a surprisingly ancient pedigree — they are the oldest of Japan's recorded snacks. Dark green kusamochi, made with mugwort or cudweed, was served at court ceremonies in 8th century Heian (now Kyoto). Heian was the first of Japan's many early capitals to have lasted for longer than a century — in fact, over a thousand years.

4. Kuzumochi (arrowroot mochi)

Under wisteria
Not as vulgar as I thought,
These Edo pastries

Not a "true" mochi, as it's made from arrowroot powder rather than rice flour, Kuzumochi are milky-white glutinous cubes, often served with soybean powder which adds a refreshing bitterness. First made in the north-western suburbs of Edo (Tokyo), a region famous for its wisterias.

15. Kuzuyaki (grilled arrowroot mochi)

Watch out, that first bite
Is as brief as the summer —
Blink and it's gone

The rivalry between Kyoto and Edo, Japan's twin capitals, extended, of course, to culinary matters, with Kyoto cuisine widely regarded as the more refined one. Accordingly, the Kyoto version of the arrowroot mochi has a subtle, delicate flavour, with a thin, biting crust that hides a refreshing coolness, ideal for Kyoto's scorching summer.

16. Warabimochi (bracken starch mochi)

Weary traveller
Rest your feet in cool water -
Now I come to you

Made from the powdered rhizome of brackens, Warabimochi was a summer specialty of inns along the Tokaido highway, linking Edo and Kyoto — but these days, it's being sold from small trucks that plod the narrow streets of Kyoto and Osaka, similar to ice cream trucks. To prevent from hardening, this mochi should be stored under cold water.

17. Kagami Mochi (mirror mochi)

Off to the battle!
I have my sword and armour
And food for a day

Mochi, a basic ration food in war times, carries as much significance and symbolism in samurai tradition as "daily bread" in the West. One of the most sacred traditions is *kagamibiraki,* "breaking the mirror" — sharing of a week-old Kagami Mochi to mark the start of a New Year, or the first training day in the martial arts dojo.

18. Daifukumochi

The bells of Toji
Ring out the arrival of
Emperor's guests

What most people worldwide think of when you mention mochi are actually Daifuku — balls of mochi dough filled with red bean paste. One of the best shops selling these is near Toji in Kyoto — one of the twin ancient temples that used to stand on both sides of Suzaku Avenue — the road leading to the Imperial Palace.

19. Ankoromochi (reversed mochi)

Don't speak of demons
All I want to ward off now
Is the summer heat

A nugget of mochi dough wrapped in red bean paste, Ankoromochi was traditionally eaten in the hottest days of summer, not only for its cooling properties, but also because it was believed to ward off evil Spirits, gathering around this time for the Festival of the Dead.

20. Sakuramochi

Death and rebirth
The rains of March taste like tears -
Both sweet and salty

One of several types of *Chimaki* — mochi wrapped in leaves — Sakuramochi is eaten not in the sakura-viewing season but in early March, when the pickled cherry leaves are at their best. Opinions differ on whether one should eat the leaf, or just savour its aroma while biting into the soft mochi dough.

21. Uiromochi

There are four seasons -
How can that be when I have
Five on my plate

People of Japan have a slight obsession with their "unique" four seasons —
understandable if compared to their semi-tropical Asian neighbours, but
verging on ridiculous when boasted to visitors from Europe or northern parts of
America. Uiro is a subtle sweet, halfway between mochi and jelly, and usually
comes in an odd number of colours and flavours — three or five.

22. Minazuki

One, two, three turn-arounds
My soul is now as pure as
These hydrangeas

Though from a distance they may look like slices of western-style cakes, Minazuki are ancient sweets made of Uiro topped with red beans in jelly. They are traditionally eaten during the summer purification ritual *Nagoshi-no-harae,* where priests have to walk through a ring of straw in a specific combination of steps.

23. Manju

All life is sacred
Red beans instead of red meat —
Decreed the Buddha

Manju are, in essence, the same as Chinese *Mantou* buns. However, in Chinese original, they were filled with pork and other meats. The vegetarian Zen monks who brought it from China replaced meat with red bean paste and other vegetable fillings. There are now as many varieties of manju as there are of mochi, both sweet and savoury.

24. Joyo Manju

The Moon is too bright —
I can't see any rabbits
Only a white ball

One of the most popular varieties of Manju, Joyo Manju is made with addition of grated yam paste. The result is both glutinous and fluffy, silkier and lighter than usual dough. Two common shapes for this sweet are either a simple white ball, or a white rabbit, like the one Japanese see in the Moon.

25. Kurogoma Manju

Pickles — hundred yen
Fresh strawberries — a thousand
Sightseeing is free

Black sesame is one of the three most popular traditional sweets flavouring after Azuki and Green Tea. The black sesame manju are lightly roasted, to get a glistening crispy outer shell around a raven-black dough packed with sesame flavour. There's an old stall selling these at Kyoto's famous Nishiki Market.

26. Dango

Don't make fun of me
I wear hair like this because
I thought you liked it

Dango are small mochi balls, often grilled, and served, several at a time, on skewers, with sweet sauce. *O-dango* is a bun as a hairstyle, either single or double, with the double *odango* made particularly famous, both in and outside Japan, by the eponymous heroine of Sailor Moon manga and anime series.

27. Yuki Ichigo

A single green leaf
Peeking from under the snow —
Too late or too early?

One of the many East-meets-West fusion sweets sold in convenience stores, Yuki Ichigo — Snow Strawberry — is among my all-time favourites: a single strawberry on a piece of shortcake, covered with whipped cream, and wrapped in snow-white or light pink mochi, it has quickly become one of the symbols of Japanese winter.

28. Zenzai

Round and round it goes
Is it the machine squeaking
Or the old lady?

Sweetened red beans are also consumed in a form of soup or porridge,
variously known (depending on thickness and occasion)
as *oshiruko* or *zenzai.* Zenzai is served with mochi, and is believed to have
powerful magical properties. The ubiquitous red bean paste is still often made
in tiny workshops, by machines as ancient as the ladies that operate them.

29. Anmitsu

The lights of Ginza!
I can't afford anything
But it's fun to watch

Anmitsu is a modern fusion dessert, invented in 1930s in a café in Ginza. Made of agar cubes, red bean paste, soft mochi and fresh fruit, Anmitsu is as extravagant as the streets where it was born — Tokyo's most luxurious shopping district. Its older form, Mitsumame, differed by having boiled beans instead of the more expensive paste.

Yakigashi — Baked goods

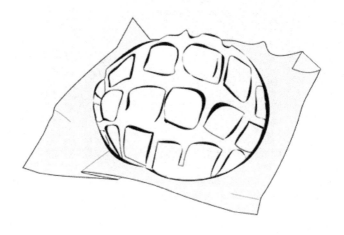

30. Melonpan

The pilgrims gathered
At the Asakusa gates
Dance the boogie-woogie

The melonpan — a sweet bun covered with criss-crossed cookie dough — is a quintessential Japanese baked product, to which all other confectionery is compared. The best ones, in my opinion, are sold at the gates of Asakusa Shrine in Tokyo: hot from the oven, perfectly crisp and the size of an Olympic discus. The tiny shop is instantly recognizable due to the unceasing blaring of "Tokyo Boogie-woogie".

31. Anpan

Ah! How brave you are
Protecting everyone's dreams
Little bun-head man

Anpan was one of the first modern Japanese sweet breads, invented by an out-of-work samurai in early Meiji period. Contrary to the name ("azuki bean bread") it can be made with any number of fillings. Anpanman, a super-hero made out of the anpan, has been one of the most popular children's characters since the 1970s.

32. Imagawayaki

White bean or read bean
The machine doesn't care
The rattling goes on

Machine-made in cast iron forms, Imagawayaki are two discs of waffle dough wrapped around a sweet filling. There's a stall deep in the bowels of Kyoto Station that sells both red-bean and white-bean paste fillings. There's always a queue of lively old ladies waiting for the treat.

33. Taiyaki

Sun glints on the scales
Eat from head or from the tail?
Wars were fought for less

Taiyaki is a type of Imagawayaki in the shape of a sea bream, ubiquitous in the city streets. Apparently, there was once a big controversy over whether one should eat it from the head or from the tail, and whether the filling should reach the tail or not.

34. Dorayaki (Mikasa)

Burning the dead grass
On top of sacred mountain
Roast to perfection

The Dorayaki pancakes, stuffed with red bean paste or custard cream, are said to resemble the shape of the Mikasa Mountain near Nara. Every January, the dead grass on the mountain is burned in a centuries-old ritual called, aptly, Yamayaki - "Mountain Baking".

35. Monaka

"Full moon in autumn" —
No need to know old poems
To taste the sweetness

Although it looks like a wafer, the outer shell of Monaka is actually mochi dough, rolled out thinly and grilled. The legend of the origin of its name tells of a party of Moon-viewing courtiers, reciting poetry and exclaiming *Monaka no tsuki!* — "A full moon!" — at the sight of the served cakes.

36. Amashoku

Clouds in eastern sky
What do they look like to you?
You dirty old man

Only in Japan could a cake as simple as Amashoku — a kind of basic sweet muffin — have caused so much controversy. Not only is there much confusion over whether people in the West of Japan know it as well as those in the East, but even the shape brings different associations to different people: some call it a UFO bun, but to others it's a woman's breast.

37. Yakiimo

A pile of ashes
All that remains of autumn
Are the vendors' cries

The beginning of winter in Japan is marked with wailing cries of the Yakiimo street vendors. The hot sweet potato is a complete snack on its own, sweet and mushy inside, crispy on the outside. Traditionally, the sweet potatoes were baked in piles of ashes made from fallen autumn leaves.

38. Senbei

Coins jingle in bowl
Of a wandering hermit
On the Sanjo Bridge

There is a very old shop selling Senbei — salted rice crackers — on the banks
of the Kamo River in Kyoto, next to the Sanjo Bridge. The bridge has stood on
this spot at least since the 16th century, and the bulbous pillar ornaments are still
all original, as are some of the pillars. As it's a popular strolling spot, the bridge
is frequented by itinerant beggar monks.

39. Arare

Is it still snowing?
Pour me another glass, boss
Not going home yet!

Arare, named after hail or snow pellets, are the smallest variety of senbei, and what is most often sold in the West as "Japanese rice crackers". Once served at the shrine festivals, nowadays they are commonly used as beer snacks, in the same way that peanuts or wasabi peas (which are themselves a type of arare) are eaten in pubs.

40. Soba Boro (Buckwheat Cookies)

The grinding of stone wheels
Resounding through city streets
Like feet on gravel

Soba, buckwheat noodles, perhaps more than anything else, is the taste — and smell — of the narrow streets of Kyoto. The dark flour is ground in stone mills at the back of the noodle shops, in a way not very different to what it must have been when the city was first established. The distinct "Boro" cookie baked of this flour is the perfect dessert after the hearty noodle soup.

Yogashi — Western style sweets

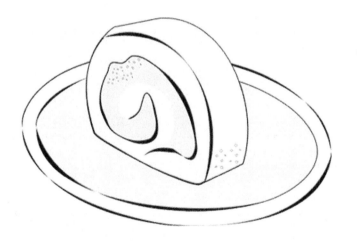

41. Castella

The guests from the West
Have brought us many gifts
Some good and some bad

Nagasaki is a city formed through Japan's interactions with the West. Long before the Bomb, it was a thriving international trading harbour, with bustling Dutch, Portuguese and Chinese enclaves. The foreigners left many marks on the city, not least in its cuisine. Castella is a sponge cake of Portuguese origin, refined to perfection by Nagasaki chefs.

42. Konpeito (Confetti)

Thank you for coming
We'll take guns, silk and candy
You can keep the rest

The Portuguese arrived in Japan seeking trade and potential Christian converts. The Japanese were only interested in the former. Among the goods obtained through the "Nanban Trade", the most appreciated were gunpowder weapons, Chinese silk and new foods, including sugar candy. The *konpeito* candy is still given as a parting gift by the Imperial Family.

43. Aruheito (Hard Candy)

A box of jewels
How quickly they disappear
Like rain in summer

Another Portuguese gift, aruheito are hard boiled sugar candies, often made to resemble little pebbles or pieces of jewellery. In the hot and humid rainy season in June, the puddles on the pavement disappear in plumes of vapour mere minutes after the rain stops.

44. Sakuma Drops

What's on TV now?
Some old black-and-white cartoon
Let's watch with grandpa

Distinctive tin boxes of fruit juice drops made by Sakuma Confectionery remained largely the same since their introduction in 1908. The only thing that changes is the label, often used to market popular anime or other pop culture events. The drops famously appeared in the "Grave of the Fireflies" animated movie — and were subsequently released with a commemorative label designed by Studio Ghibli.

45. Siberia

Empire's glory
Say farewell to our brave boys —
They're not going back

Another old treat brought back by a Ghibli movie ("The Wind Rises"), Siberia - a combination of castella cake and azuki jelly - was popular in early 20th century, before World War II. The name is supposedly inspired by the 1905 Russo-Japanese war. The recent wave of nostalgia brought record sales to a small bakery in Yokohama harbour, which has been making Siberia since 1916.

46. Ringoame (Candy Apple)

Wasshoi! Wasshoi! Wa —
This shrine's too heavy for me
I need more candy

In Japan, candy apples are sold almost exclusively during the *matsuri* — shrine festivals. Matsuri is the time to eat the kind of food one normally wouldn't associate with Japan: fried, fatty, unhealthy, but most of all — simple and fun. Other fruit is also available in this form, depending on season — strawberries and oranges are the most popular.

47. Shuu Kuriimu (Cream Puff)

Discounts for the fans
The deal for today is
Strawberry heaven

There's a choux créme stall (belonging to the Beard Papa franchise) near the main exit of the Akihabara Station in Tokyo, in the kingdom of geeks, nerds and otaku. These days, the smell of the freshly baked cream puffs pulls me in stronger than the scantily-clad cosplayers who parade this area...

48. Monburan (Mont Blanc)

How unexpected
Climbing a mountain in snow —
I find summer sun

An old French dessert embraced wholeheartedly in Japan, since its introduction in 1930s it's become a recognizable staple of every Japanese patisserie in the world. There are now many more varieties of Mont Blanc than just the traditional chestnut cream — sweet potatoes, pumpkin, green tea, or fruit cream.

49. Roll Cake

The mighty lion
In dreams, in reality
All it hunts is milk

The Swiss Roll is one of those unassuming cakes that gained unexpected popularity in Showa Japan. Filled with whipped cream and fruit, or flavoured with more traditional additives like matcha or chestnuts, the soft and fluffy roll cake somehow reminds me of a rolled-up, sleeping kitten.

50. Soufflé Cheesecake

A drunken sailor
Falls asleep in a snow bank
Softer than pillow

I was unable to figure out why the Japanese cheesecake is so different from anywhere else. Variously known as soufflé or cotton cheesecake in the West, it is a fluffy mixture of egg meringue and cream cheese, with texture of a sponge pillow. Dairy is still a rare delicacy in Japan, and most local cheese comes from the dairy farms in Hokkaido - not far from Russia.

51. Rusk

Coffee's expensive
But you can't dunk a biscuit
In a metal can

A can of sugary coffee from a vending machine costs around 100 yen. A cup of coffee in a café can ring up six times that. In the overcrowded, busy Japan, you pay more for a quiet place to sit and sip your drink, rather than for the coffee itself. Biscotti-like rusks are a surprising staple in Japan's bakeries and patisseries.

52. Baumkuchen

The trees of Peace Park
Remember only soft winds
Rustling the leaves

The Japanese embrace food from any country, if it's good enough for their taste. The humble Central European baumkuchen takes pride of place among the favourite souvenirs. It was first introduced to Japan at the Hiroshima Prefectural Exhibition Hall — a building better known as the Atomic Bomb Dome, in Hiroshima Peace Memorial Park. Only 170 trees in all of Hiroshima survived the bombing.

53. Strawberry Shortcake

If being too old
Means I'm like this Christmas Cake
I don't want to be young

A rather terrible tradition claimed that Japanese women who are still single when they're 26 years old, are as past their prime as an unsold Christmas Cake, stale and unappetizing after December 25th. Luckily, this tradition seems to be dying out these days — good for women, and good for the delicious cakes.

54. Giri Choco

The chocolates I got
Were not of the cheapest kind
What does it mean?

Another odd Japanese tradition is the *Giri Choco* — an obligatory gift of chocolates from women/girls to men/boys on Valentine's Day. Unlike *Honmei Choco,* which conveys hidden romantic feelings, *Giri Choco* is aimed at friends, class-mates or co-workers with no romance involved. It is usually quite cheap, with the more expensive varieties reserved for that Special One.

55. Purin (Créme Caramel)

Open your lunch box
On the first day of school —
Delicious wobble

It may come as a surprise to learn that the standard custard pudding with caramel sauce is a nostalgia food in Japan. It's been a childhood favourite, and part of packed school lunches since the 1960s, and Japanese baby boomers still remember it fondly as one of the first sweet snacks to break the monotony of post-war rationing.

56. CalorieMate

We need energy
To build the modern Japan!
But I'm so tired...

The Japanese Miracle Decade of the 1980s brought many culinary inventions that were supposed to fuel the average salarymen in their quest for wealth and prestige. Next to the new energy drinks like Pocari Sweat, a cookie for the new era appeared: a shortbread created in a laboratory, filled with nutrients and minerals, your new best friend in work and leisure — CalorieMate.

57. Pocky

Yes, yes, Pocky Girls,
What is this wonderful sound?
It's calling me in

Like Pocari Sweat, Pocky sticks were one of the symbols of "otaku Japan" in the late 1990s. It was the era in which the Western world — me included — truly discovered Japanese pop culture: manga, anime, video games and pop music. At the time, I was a huge fan of a legendary, best-selling girls-band *Morning Musume* and "Pocky Girls" was a tune they sang in a Pocky TV ad.

58. Tokyo Banana

Tokyo holiday
Of all the things to bring back
This sweet mushy thing?

Kyoto has *Yatsuhashi*. Kanazawa has *Yubeshi.* Tokyo has long searched for its own *miyagegashi* — a sweet that is typically bought as a souvenir. It wasn't until 1990s that a baking company came up with an unlikely hit — Tokyo Banana, a banana puree wrapped in sponge cake. What it has to do with Tokyo is anyone's guess — but perhaps its idiosyncrasy is the secret to popularity of a snack now associated with the greatest metropolis in the world.

59. Kininaru Ringo

The trees bloom in pink
More precious and exquisite
Than cherryblossom

Another example of modern *miyagegashi* — this one is a whole apple baked in a pastry shell. It represents Aomori, region that since the 1870s produces most of Japan's apples. Hirosaki was once a capital city of the region, and it's castle grounds are the most popular cherry blossom viewing spot in northern Japan.

60. Konbini Snacks

Don't disturb me, please
I won't sleep until I know
What happened next

There are always hundreds of varieties of snacks, both sweet and savoury, on the shelves of local convenience stores, or "konbini". Regional, seasonal, associated with holidays, tied-in with pop-culture merchandise... A common sight in a konbini late at night are rows of students standing by the newspaper stands, reading the latest installment of their favourite manga.

Hyoka — Chilled desserts

61. Aisu Kyuri

The hills are on fire!
No, it's just the mist rising
In fields of shiso

Alright, so it's not really a sweet, but there can be no summer in Kyoto without
a visit to a northern suburb of Ohara, to try its specialty — ice-cold cucumbers,
gently pickled in seaweed, until in taste and texture they resemble a delicious,
savoury ice cream. Ohara is also famous for its temples, and fields of
purple *shiso,* an aromatic herb.

62. Kakigori

Secrets of happiness:
Stare at the sea in silence
Waiting for shaved ice

The height of Japanese summer would be unbearable without a bowl of freshly shaved ice, topped with condensed milk and syrup, sold from a street stand. It's no accident that making of (and eating) perfect *Kakigori* features as one of the secrets of enlightenment in one of my favourite Japanese movies of all time, Naoko Ogigami's "Megane".

63. Ujikintoki

Across Uji bridge
The Lady of the West Wing
Dips spoon in a bowl

Although I doubt that the heroine of the Tale of Genji got to eat Ujikintoki — a dessert of shaved ice, Uji green tea and adzuki beans — it's probable she ate an early "prototype", *kezurihi* — ice scraped from blocks with sharp blade, with sweet vine syrup. It wasn't until the industrialization of the Meiji period that *kakigori* became the cheap summer staple it is today.

64. Mizuyokan

Chestnuts like pebbles
Gleaming in frozen river
Memory of winter

Mizuyokan is a commoner's version of the artisan Kingyoku, sold in thick blocks of agar jelly flavoured with red bean. Other yokans exist, made with matcha or chestnut, sometimes with bits of fruit or nuts suspended inside. They may not be as elaborate and beautiful as their courtly counterparts, but, sold chilled, make for a great alternative to other summer desserts.

65. Kinako Ice Cream

On rain-dappled street
Please, can I make a photo —
Oh, just a tourist

Ice cream made with kinako — soybean flour — is served in a delightful café in an old building just off Gion's main thoroughfare. Gion is Kyoto's geisha district, and one of the few places where you can still "spot" an authentic "willow girl". Unlike tourists or models in disguise, they stride purposefully on, not stopping to admire views — or for photos.

66. Sofutokuriimu (Soft Serve)

How do flowers taste?
I will tell you as soon as
I'm finished with these

Soft-serve ice cream has been elevated to an art form in Japan. There's not a place that wouldn't have their own local, seasonal flavours. Anything can be made into a *sofutokuriimu* flavour: flowers, wasabi, natto, seafood, squid ink, even snake venom. The only limit seems to be the imagination of the vendors.

67. Monaka Ice Cream

Still dripping with steam
Goblin hides in the forest
Waiting for the train

Like Monaka Mochi, Monaka Ice Cream is a sandwich of wafer-thin dough, except filled with ice-cream. Most famous are made by Morinaga, but I'm partial to the azuki-filled ones sold from Glico's 17 Ice vending machines, like the one at the Kurama Onsen train station, north of Kyoto. The forests around Kurama hot spring resort were a famous hiding place of *Tengu*, the long-nosed goblins.

68. Shirokuma

When the ashes fall
A gleaming snow ball is good
To rest weary eyes

Kagoshima is a city of grey. Perched next to an active volcano, it is showered daily with ash and cinders. Perhaps this is why the sweet makers of Kagoshima came up with Shirokuma — "Polar Bear" — a cup of shaved ice covered with condensed milk and fruit to form a little glistening orb of bright colours, refreshing in the sea of ashes.

69. Parfait

A horn of plenty
Taller than Tokyo Tower
Gentle happiness

What the Japanese call "parfait" is the pinnacle of their dessert-making ingenuity. A fusion of all of ancient traditions and Western influences: a tower of soft serve ice cream, agar jellies, mochi, red bean paste, bits of rusk and shortcake, fresh fruit and syrups.

The slogan of Karafuneya, the greatest and most famous parfait shop in Kyoto, with nearly a hundred varieties, proudly exclaims: *"Karafuneya — filled with gentle happiness."*

70. Kyogashi - Kyoto Sweets

Cellophane rustle
On pavement splattered with rain
Old woman's footsteps

Our favourite Wagashi shop in Shimogyo-ku, Kyoto

Printed in Great Britain
by Amazon

55712066R00046